Human Body Systems

The Nervous System

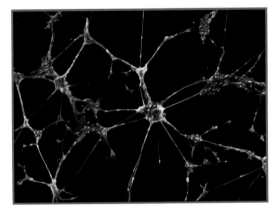

by Rebecca Olien

Consultant:
Marjorie Hogan, MD
Pediatrician
Hennepin County Medical Center
Minneapolis, Minnesota

Capstone
press

Mankato, Minnesota

Bridgestone Books are published by Capstone Press,
151 Good Counsel Drive, P.O. Box 669, Mankato, Minnesota 56002.
www.capstonepress.com

Library of Congress Cataloging-in-Publication Data
Olien, Rebecca.
 The nervous system / by Rebecca Olien.
  p. cm.—(Bridgestone books. Human body systems)
 Summary: "Learn about the job of the nervous system, problems that may come up, and how to
keep the system healthy"—Provided by publisher.
 Includes bibliographical references and index.
 ISBN-13: 978-0-7368-5412-2 (hardcover)
 ISBN-10: 0-7368-5412-6 (hardcover)
 1. Nervous system—Juvenile literature. I. Title. II. Series: Bridgestone books. Human body systems.
QP361.5O52 2006
612.8—dc22   2005021153

Editorial Credits

Amber Bannerman, editor; Bobbi J. Dey, designer; Kelly Garvin, photo researcher/photo editor

Photo Credits

BananaStock, Ltd., 4
Capstone Press/Karon Dubke, cover (girl), 12, 16
Corbis/Michael Freeman, 6 (nervous system)
Getty Images Inc./Brooklyn Productions, 20
Photo Researchers Inc./John M. Daugherty, 6 (hand); Mehau Kulyk/Science Photo Library, 8; Science
    Photo Library/Pasieka, cover (nerves); Science Source, 18
Visuals Unlimited/Dr. Michael Delannoy, 1; Ralph Hutchings, 14

1 2 3 4 5 6 11 10 09 08 07 06

Table of Contents

How You Feel

Brrr! You can feel a cold ice cream cone against your tongue because of your nerves. Nerves send signals to your brain to tell you the ice cream is freezing.

Your nervous system helps you feel things and keeps your heart beating. It works with all your body systems to help you learn things, such as how to read and do math. Your brain, **spinal cord**, and nerves make up your nervous system.

◄ Nerves send signals to tell you ice cream is cold.

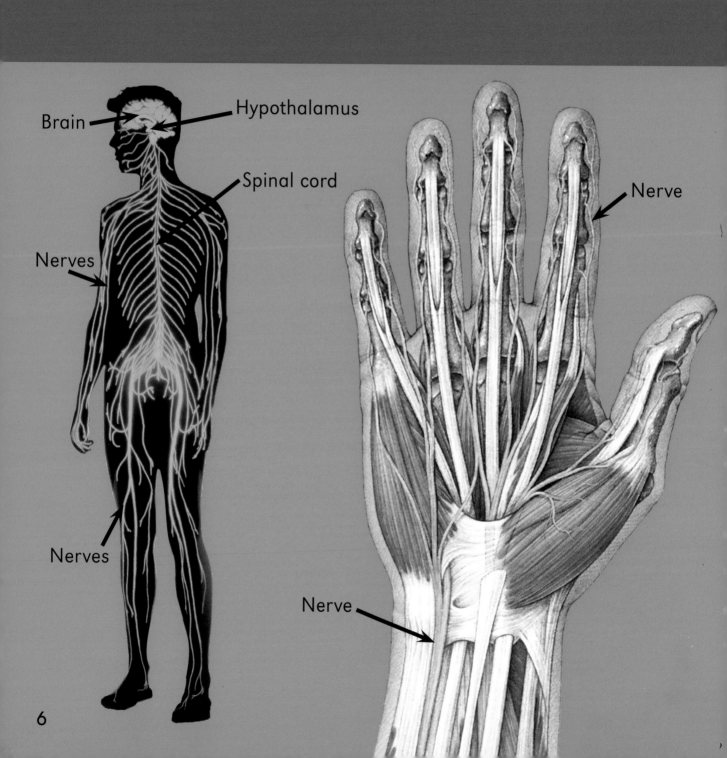

Brain

Hypothalamus

Spinal cord

Nerves

Nerves

Nerve

Nerve

6

Message System

Your nervous system is the message system of your body. Messages travel as electric signals along a pathway of nerves. Nerves branch out to every part of your body.

The nervous system is made up of three systems. Your brain and spinal cord make up your central nervous system. The peripheral nervous system includes nerves that connect to the brain and spinal cord. The brain's hypothalamus helps regulate the autonomic nervous system. It controls things that happen automatically, like digestion.

◀ Nerves are found all over your body, including in your hands.

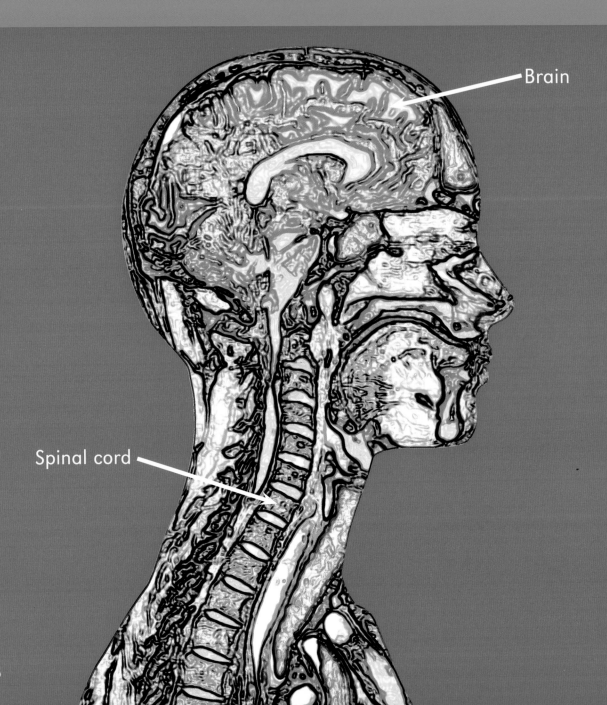

Brain

Spinal cord

Central Nervous System

The central nervous system controls the whole nervous system. Within this system is the brain, the control center of your body. Your brain receives information from places like your eyes, skin, and tongue. Then, your brain sends signals to tell your body what to do.

Feel the bumps on the back of your neck. They are part of your spine. Inside your spine is your spinal cord. Your spinal cord starts at your neck and stops a little more than halfway down your back. Your spinal cord is the main highway for signals to move to and from the brain.

◄ The central nervous system's brain and spinal cord are color-enhanced in this image.

Nerve Cell

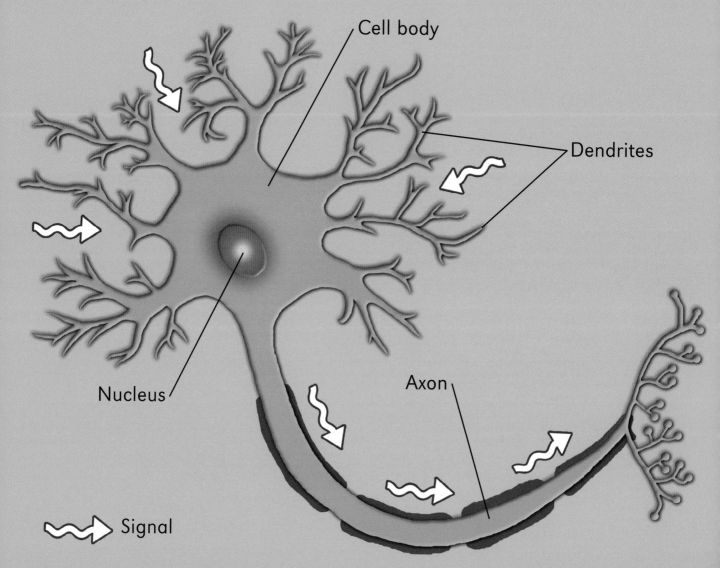

Cell body

Dendrites

Nucleus

Axon

Signal

Nerves

Nerves run from the top of your head to the tips of your toes. They look like bundles of thin, gray threads. A countless number of nerves are in your body.

Nerves are made of **cells**. Most nerve cells have a cell body, an **axon**, and many **dendrites**. Inside the cell body is a **nucleus**, or control center. The short dendrites receive signals. The long axons send signals to other nerve cells, then to the brain. Electric signals are passed through the body from nerve cell to nerve cell.

◄ Nerve cells carry signals throughout the body.

Nerves and the Senses

Nerves use sensors to gather information. Sensors tell your brain what is happening outside of your body. Each of the five senses has special sensors.

You can see a bucket of popcorn because sensors in your eyes send a signal to your brain. Your touch sensors tell you the popcorn feels rough. You can smell popcorn because sensors in your nose send a signal. Sensors in your ears send the sound of crunching. Taste bud sensors tell you the popcorn tastes salty and buttery.

◄ Nerves help you eat and watch TV at the same time.

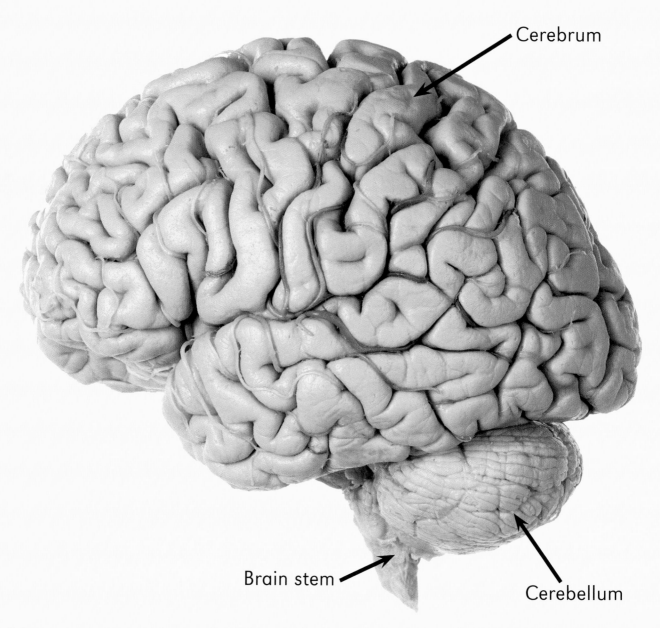

Cerebrum

Brain stem

Cerebellum

Parts of the Brain

The **cerebrum** is the largest part of the brain. It is full of wrinkles. Learning, imagining, and memory take place in the cerebrum.

The brain stem is at the bottom of the brain, right above the neck. It connects the brain to the spinal cord. The brain stem manages breathing, heartbeat, and the flow of messages from the rest of the body.

Your **cerebellum** is just above the brain stem. It's about the size of a tennis ball. This part of your brain regulates balance and controls the way muscles move.

◀ The brain's cerebrum, cerebellum, and brain stem each have different functions.

Nerves and Muscles

To move your body, your nerves and muscles work together. You think about moving, and then your brain sends signals through your nerves. Your nerves deliver these signals to make your muscles squeeze. As a muscle squeezes, it pulls, dragging the bone along with it.

You don't have to think about making some of your muscles work. These muscles work automatically. Nerves signal the heart to pump blood and keep it flowing. Other nerves signal digestive muscles to move food.

◄ Nerves send electric signals to your arm and hand, helping you throw a ball.

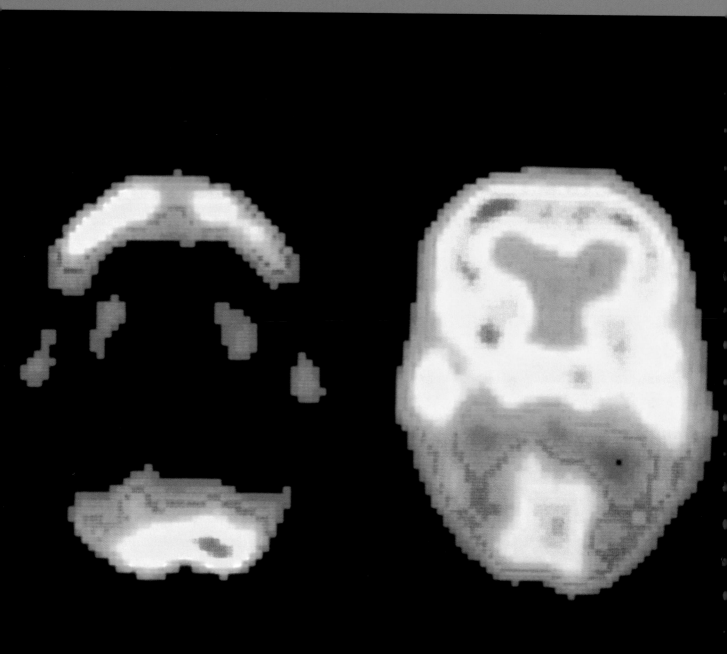

18

Diseases and Drugs

Some diseases damage nerves. Parkinson's disease kills nerves that control muscles. Alzheimer's disease attacks nerves in the brain, causing memory loss.

Alcohol and drug use also harm nerves. Drugs change the way nerves work, and can destroy nerves. Every time a drug is taken, more nerves are damaged. These nerves may never work right again.

◄ The black areas in the brain on the left show damage to brain cells from Alzheimer's disease. The brain on the right is healthy.

Keeping Healthy

To keep your nervous system healthy, good food and enough sleep go a long way. Eating healthy fruits and veggies gives your nervous system energy. Sleep gives your brain and nerves much needed rest.

Safety gear also keeps your nervous system healthy. A bicycle helmet protects your brain if you fall. A seatbelt keeps you from bumping your head in the car. Keep yourself healthy, and your nervous system will stay well.

◄ Seatbelts help keep you safe while you're riding in a vehicle.

Glossary

axon (AK-sahn)—the part of a nerve cell that sends signals

cell (SEL)—a tiny part of the body; nerve cells send and receive signals.

cerebellum (ser-ah-BELL-uhm)—the part of the brain that controls balance and the way muscles move

cerebrum (ser-EE-bruhm)—the main part of the brain where thinking, feeling, and remembering take place

dendrite (DEN-drite)—a branch on a nerve cell that receives signals

nucleus (NOO-klee-uhss)—the center part of a cell; the nucleus is also known as the control center.

spinal cord (SPINE-uhl KORD)—a thick cord of nerves that carries signals to the rest of the nerves in the body; the spinal cord carries signals both to and from the brain.

Read More

DeGezelle, Terri. *Your Brain.* The Bridgestone Science Library. Mankato, Minn.: Bridgestone Books, 2002.

Royston, Angela. *Why Do I Get a Toothache?: And Other Questions about Nerves.* Body Matters. Chicago: Heinemann Library, 2003.

Internet Sites

FactHound offers a safe, fun way to find Internet sites related to this book. All of the sites on FactHound have been researched by our staff.

Here's how:

1. Visit *www.facthound.com*
2. Type in this special code **0736854126** for age-appropriate sites. Or enter a search word related to this book for a more general search.
3. Click on the **Fetch It** button.

FactHound will fetch the best sites for you!

Index